TIME CHRONICLES

Tyler:

His Story

Written by Roderick Hunt
and illustrated by Alex Brychta

OXFORD

Before you begin …

Dear Reader,

Before you begin this Chronicle, you should know that Biff, Chip, Kipper and friends have become Time Runners. They are based in the Time Vault, a place that exists outside time. Their mission is to travel back in time to defeat the Virans.

Virans are dark energy in human form. Their aim is to destroy history and so bring chaos to the future.

The Time Runners have to be brave and self-reliant. They have a Zaptrap, which is a device to capture the Virans. They also have a Link, which is a bit like a mobile phone disguised as a yo-yo. The Link lets them communicate with the Time Vault. Apart from that, when on a mission, they are very much on their own!

Theodore Mortlock
Time Guardian

A science lecture, early 1800s

This was an age of discovery! Scientists were making important discoveries about the way the world works. They began to realise that everything in the world is made up of a few simple elements, like oxygen. This news gripped people's imagination. Everyone wanted to learn about science!

Chapter 1

"It's a bomb!" yelled Tyler. "It's going to blow the place up. Get everyone out!"

He raced towards the line of fizzing flame and sparks.

"Stamp on it!" he shouted. "It's a fuse!"

In front of him was an open trap door. Then he was falling into a dark space. His body twisted. His arms jerked. As Tyler hit the ground he felt an agonizing pain.

"Tyler!" said Wilma gently. "Wake up!"

Tyler was asleep in an armchair in the library with a book on his lap. He opened his eyes. "I was having a bad dream," he said.

He began to rub his leg. "I get this ache in me leg, ever since the accident."

Wilma frowned. What accident? Tyler had come to the Time Vault from the past. Who was he, and what was his story?

Kipper was messing about in Tyler's techno-chair. He sped through the library as Nadim appeared in the doorway, carrying a chessboard set out in a game that was half-finished.

"Whoops!" shouted Kipper. The techno-chair skidded. Nadim sprang aside, but the chess pieces flew off on to the floor.

"Kipper! You idiot!" Nadim shouted. "You've ruined our game."

Kipper jumped out of the chair and began to pick up the chess pieces.

"And I was winning!" complained Nadim.

"Don't worry, Nadim," said Tyler. "I'll put them back. I can remember where the pieces went."

Tyler's words made Nadim even crosser. "You're too clever by half, Tyler," he shouted. "And Kipper! You're just a pest. Now say sorry!"

Kipper threw the chess pieces back on the floor. "I won't! You're a pain, Nadim."

"Hey! Stop it!" said Wilma. "We don't want any trouble in the Time Vault."

Chapter 2

Biff and Wilf were playing pool in the games room. Biff took a wild shot. The cue ball flew into the air. There was a tearing sound as Biff's cue ripped a long tear in the cloth.

"Biff!" shouted Wilf. "That was stupid!"

"Don't call me stupid," said Biff, hotly.

At that moment, the Link in Biff's pocket buzzed. Wilf's Link went off too. "An emergency?" Biff gasped.

The Link was a hi-tech communication device. Biff snapped hers open. Wilma had sent everyone a message. It read, "Urgent meeting. Library. In 10 minutes."

Chapter 3

When everyone had arrived, Wilma said, "This messing about has to stop. We're beginning to fall out."

She was right. They had been having fun. Things had got out of hand. Kipper stared at the floor. Biff looked uncomfortable.

Wilf didn't agree. "Come on, Wilma!" he protested. "We're just letting off steam. It's boring with nothing to do."

"Boring!" shouted Tyler. "You know nothing! Try living like I did once, with no proper home. No books, TV, computers, mobile phones. Imagine no place to wash yerself or go to the loo. Imagine huddling in a damp, stinking shelter with no bed to sleep in. Imagine just sitting there, cold and hungry, staring at the rain all day. Then you'd know what boring means!"

They looked at Tyler in surprise. Wilf hung his head. "Sorry, Tyler, I didn't know."

"My mother used to get cross if I said I was bored," said Tyler.

"You haven't spoken about your mother or father before," said Wilma, gently.

Tyler sniffed. "That's 'cos I'm an orphan. Both my parents are dead."

There was an awkward silence. Tyler went on. "If I tell you my story, maybe you will see how lucky you are."

This is the story Tyler told them.

Chapter 4

My mother was beautiful. She was French. My father was an officer in the British Navy. He was killed at sea in 1801. It broke my mother's heart, 'cos after that, she fell ill and took to her bed.

The night she died, she was having a job to breathe. I ran to get a doctor. I banged on his door and sobbed, "Please come! My mother's ill. She needs help."

I'll never forget what he said to me.

"I'm eating my supper! If she's that
French woman, I'll come in the morning."
And he shut the door.

But he never came, and by the next day I
was an orphan. I was nine years old.

After my mother died, the landlord said
we owed him rent. I had no money so he
took my mother's jewellery. Then he told me
to get out of the house.

I had no one to turn to. I had nowhere to go. I packed a bag with some clothes and a few of my mother's things. Suddenly, I was homeless, like a street urchin.

It's not easy to find places to sleep in London. The first night, I huddled in a doorway. But a drunk woman saw me and grabbed me by the throat.

"I'll 'ave that bag," she hissed.

Luckily, I was wearing all my clothes to keep warm. But she stole everything else.

I was always hungry. I ate what people threw out, half-eaten or gone rotten.

I soon met the street urchins. They wore rags. Most of them stank. They had bad teeth and filthy, matted hair. They used to steal things to survive.

One of them told me the best place to sleep was up on a roof. "It's safer up high," he said. "You can keep warm if you find a hot chimney to warm your back."

Every day, I used to go to the big market at Covent Garden. Stuff from all over the world came up the Thames by boat and was sold at the market – silks, spices, china, coloured glass, ivory, even things like monkeys and parrots.

I tried to keep myself clean and tidy. I didn't want to look like a street urchin. They stole things and people chased them away.

I did jobs round the market. I might get paid with an apple or a stale cake. Once, a woman gave me a farthing. It was not much, but I bought a broken comb.

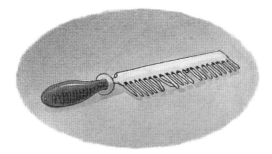

Chapter 5

One day, there was bad news. It was 18th May 1803. Britain declared war on France. Napoleon's army was getting ready to invade England.

I was reading about this in a newspaper, when a man said, "I can't read so I'll give you a farthing to read that to me."

"I'll read it to you for a penny!" I said.

"How about a halfpenny?" he replied.

So I did. It was easy money!

It was hard to keep warm at night. One day I stopped outside a big building called the Royal Foundation. It was where people went to read books and learn things. People were outside queuing up to hear a science lecture about magnets.

"Is the lecture free?" I asked a man.

"Yes, anyone can go in," he said.

"Good," I thought. "If they let me in I'll have somewhere warm to sit for an hour."

I went to the lecture. I was amazed at the things magnets do. The way they have a force field, or make a swinging metal arrow point to the north. After that, I went to other lectures. One was on stars and planets.

Sometimes, I went into the library to read. But on some days the place was shut. Important people like scientists, explorers or writers would meet there for big dinners.

I was pretty good at climbing on to the roofs of buildings by now. And at the back of the Royal Foundation, I saw a half-open window high up on the roof.

I shinned up and found I could slip through the window into the attic. It was crammed full of junk, but in the corner was a pile of dusty old curtains. At last, I had found a dry, warm place to sleep that was safe.

After a week, I began to feel brave. So one moonlit night, I crept down the narrow attic steps to explore the building.

It was like a great house that a lord might live in. It had a wide staircase with portraits on the walls. It was dark and silent but I crept like a mouse. I didn't know if anyone was living there.

Downstairs there had been a late dinner. No one had cleared away. Left-over food was still on the tables – meat, bread, jellies and fruit. I was ravenous. I began to tuck in.

But suddenly, I froze!

I heard low voices. Then the dim light of a lantern cast shadows on the wall. A man and a woman were prowling through the dark rooms! I dived under a table. My heart beat like a drum. To my surprise, they were speaking French.

I speak French. I heard words like 'flames', 'fire' and something about France. One of them said something about 'destroying science'. They used the words 'candle' and 'explosion'. It meant nothing to me.

When I was sure they had gone I crept back to the attic. It was hard to sleep. Why were two French people creeping around in the dark? Britain was at war with France, so were they secret agents or spies? Did they mean to set fire to something or blow something up?

How could I tell anyone what I had heard, and where I had heard it? Even if I did, who would believe a street urchin like me?

Chapter 6

Then I read about a big science lecture at the Royal Foundation. Famous scientists and important people were going to it. I heard that even the Prime Minister would be there.

The lecture was about oxygen, and how things need oxygen to burn. If there's no oxygen, flames go out. It was new science. People didn't know much about it.

The day of the lecture, I sneaked into the lecture hall early. It was soon full of people. A tall man ordered me out of my seat, so I crept to the front and sat on the floor.

The lecture began. The curtains had been drawn to darken the hall. Straight away, the scientist lit lots of candles. He said that oxygen was one of the elements in the air. Things like candles could not burn without it. A candle went out when there was no air. A glowing ember burst into flame when it was put into pure oxygen.

Then I remembered! The French people had said 'fire' and 'flame'. They had said 'destroy science'. They had said 'EXPLOSION'!

My heart raced. Had they been plotting to cause an explosion during the lecture?

Suddenly, a candle began to spark.

I saw it at once, a trail of dark powder running along the floor. Gunpowder! The trail led to some heavy velvet curtains behind the scientist.

The sparks from the spitting candle began to fall near the gunpowder.

My father had told me about gunpowder and how a single spark would set it off.

I knew I had to do something!

"It's a bomb!" I yelled. "It's going to blow the place up. Get everyone out!"

A spark landed on the trail of gunpowder. It hissed and fizzed like an angry snake. Flame and sparks leapt along it in less than the blink of an eye. I leapt up and raced towards it.

"Stamp on it!" I shouted.

I burst through the curtains. The fizzing trail was already close to an open trapdoor. In that instant I knew that barrels of gunpowder were in a cellar under the hall. I knew the gunpowder trail would reach them and the barrels would explode.

I dived headfirst. I slid through the trail of gunpowder and fell through the trapdoor.

"It will be a big explosion!" I thought.

I twisted in the air. Then I landed heavily on a barrel and crashed on to a stone floor.

I waited for the explosion.

My leg was bent under me. I couldn't move it. I knew it was broken. The pain was terrible.

I looked down. My hands and jacket were black. My headlong dive through the gunpowder had wiped the floor clean!

There was no explosion.

Chapter 7

Two men ran into the cellar. They grabbed my arms and ankles to carry me out. It was agony. The pain was so bad I passed out.

I woke up in a hospital run by nuns. They put my leg into two wooden splints and wrapped it round with bandages. I was angry 'cos my trouser leg had been cut off.

I wasn't able to walk again. I can't bend my leg, see. It gives way, so I fall over a lot.

Was I a hero? I saved a lot of lives that day. Did I get a medal? You'd think so.

The newspapers said that two French spies had been arrested for trying to cause explosions. Did they mention me? No! I was a street urchin!

One good thing came out of it. A boy called Michael Faraday had been at the lecture. He came to see me in the hospital. He brought food and books. We soon became friends. Later he made me a chair with wheels on so I could move about.

No one had moved while Tyler had been telling his story. No one spoke. At last Wilma broke the silence.

"What an amazing story," she said.

"Now you know why you lot are so lucky," replied Tyler. "Life wasn't easy in the past for some kids. It probably isn't easy for loads of them, even today."

Then Neena said, "Those French spies who tried to blow up the lecture. Do you think they were Virans?"

Tyler looked thoughtful. "Well, Michael Faraday thought they might have been. I'd never heard of Virans before I met him. I suppose we'll never know."

"I know one thing," said Kipper. "There has been too much messing about in the Time Vault. After supper, I'm going to settle down with a good book."

"Yeah, Kipper," said Wilf. "I believe you!"

Tyler's Mission Report

Location:	Date:
Time Vault	*Today*
Mission Status:	Viran Status:
No mission.	

Notes:

What made me tell my story? I had two reasons. First, I was mad at everyone. I mean, life in the Time Vault is so easy, but they just mess about and waste time.

And second, I come from the past. It's a strange feeling to be living over two hundred years in the future. I've come across things I simply couldn't even have imagined. So look at it from my point of view. How many things do you think were completely new to me when I arrived in the Time Vault? Put it another way – what would you miss most if you went back to 1800? Why not start in your kitchen at home?

Sign off: ....*Tyler*.........................

History: downloaded!
The Age of Science

To make a cake, we mix together ingredients such as eggs, butter, flour and sugar. As the cake cooks, the ingredients change to make the cake.

Michael Faraday doing an experiment

Everything in the world is made of ingredients called elements. There are over a hundred. You may have heard of some of them: iron, copper, calcium, helium. Water is made of two elements: hydrogen and oxygen. Almost all of the human body is made of six elements: oxygen, carbon, hydrogen, nitrogen, calcium and phosphorus.

A science lecture

Until about 250 years ago, people thought that everything was made of just four elements – earth, fire, air and water. So it was very exciting when scientists began to prove that this was not the case and elements like oxygen existed.

Oxygen was discovered by three scientists at almost the same time. The credit is given to Joseph Priestley in 1774 because he published a paper about it.

The public was so interested in discoveries like this, that scientists gave lectures and did experiments in front of large audiences of people.

Science equipment from the 1800s

For more information, see the Time Chronicles website:
www.oxfordprimary.co.uk/timechronicles

Glossary

ember *(page 28)* A small piece of glowing wood or coal taken from a dying fire. *A glowing ember burst into flame when it was put into pure oxygen.*

farthing *(page 19)* An old English coin worth one quarter of a penny. *Once, a woman gave me a farthing.*

landlord *(page 16)* Someone who owns a room, flat or house, but allows others to live there as long as they pay a monthly amount, known as 'rent'. *After my mother died, the landlord said we owed him rent.*

oxygen *(page 27)* A clear, colourless, tasteless gas. There is oxygen in the air. *If there's no oxygen, flames go out.*

splint *(page 33)* A piece of wood strapped to a broken leg to keep it straight. *They put my leg into two wooden splints and wrapped it round with bandages.*

street urchin *(page 17)* A child with no home or family. They live on the street and sleep wherever they can. *Suddenly, I was homeless, like a street urchin.*

Thesaurus: Another word for ...

prowling *(page 24)* sneaking, creeping, stalking, slinking.